Watching the Weather

Rain

Elizabeth Miles

Heinemann
LIBRARY

www.heinemann.co.uk/library

To order:
☎ Phone 44 (0) 1865 888066
▤ Send a fax to 44 (0) 1865 314091
▭ Visit the Heinemann Bookshop at www.heinemann.co.uk/library to browse our catalogue and order online.

First published in Great Britain by Heinemann Library, Halley Court, Jordan Hill, Oxford OX2 8EJ, part of Harcourt Education.
Heinemann is a registered trademark of Harcourt Education Ltd.

Editorial: Nicole Irving and Tanvi Rai
Design: Richard Parker and Celia Jones
Illustrations: Jeff Edwards
Picture Research: Rebecca Sodergren and Mica Brancic
Production: Séverine Ribierre

Originated by Dot Gradations Ltd.
Printed and bound in China by South China Printing Company

ISBN 0 431 19024 0
09 08 07 06 05
10 9 8 7 6 5 4 3 2 1

British Library Cataloguing in Publication Data
Miles, Elizabeth
    Rain. – (Watching the weather)
    551.5'77
A full catalogue record for this book is available from the British Library.

Acknowledgements
The Publishers would like to thank the following for permission to reproduce photographs: Alamy Images pp. 11, 16; Ardea/Ake Lindau p. 23; Corbis p. 6; Corbis/David Pollack p. 17; Corbis/Kevin Fleming p. 19; Corbis/Nick Hawkes; Ecoscene p. 27, Corbis/Raymond Gehman p. 13; Corbis/Sally A Morgan; Ecoscene p. 25; Corbis/William James Warren p. 5; Digital Vision p. 20; Getty Images/Image Bank p. 12; Getty Images/PhotoDisc pp. i, 22, 26; Getty Images/Stone p. 4; Harcourt Education Ltd/Tudor Photography p. 28; PA Photos/EPA pp. 18, 24; Panos Pictures/Sven Torfinn p. 21; Robert Harding Picture Library Ltd p. 7.

Cover photograph of rain falling on grass reproduced with permission of Corbis/Craig Turtle.

The Publishers would like to thank Daniel Odgen for his assistance in the preparation of this book.

Every effort has been made to contact copyright holders of any material reproduced in this book. Any omissions will be rectified in subsequent printings if notice is given to the Publishers.

The paper used to print this book comes from sustainable resources.

Contents

What is rain? 4

Where does rain come from? 6

Water in the air 8

The water cycle 10

Different kinds of rain 12

Rainfall around the world 14

Rain and the seasons 16

Who needs rain? 18

Plants in the rain 20

Animals in the rain 22

Floods 24

Acid rain 26

Project: rain diary 28

Glossary 30

Find out more 31

Index 32

Any words appearing in the text in bold, **like this**, are explained in the Glossary.

 Find out more about rain at
www.heinemannexplore.co.uk

What is rain?

Rain is water that falls from the sky. Rainwater can make us wet and make puddles on the street.

We wear raincoats and carry umbrellas on rainy days.

Rain is made up of lots of drops of water.
These are called raindrops. You can see
raindrops when they stick to the outside of
a window.

Where does rain come from?

When we see lots of clouds in the sky, we know it may rain.

Rain comes from clouds. Clouds are made of billions of tiny drops of water called **droplets**. Droplets are so small and light, they float in the air.

When water droplets join together they get big and heavy. Soon they get too heavy to float in the air. Then they fall from the cloud as raindrops.

Water in the air

When the Sun heats water on the ground, some of it rises into the air. It rises as a **gas** called **water vapour**. We cannot see water vapour in the air.

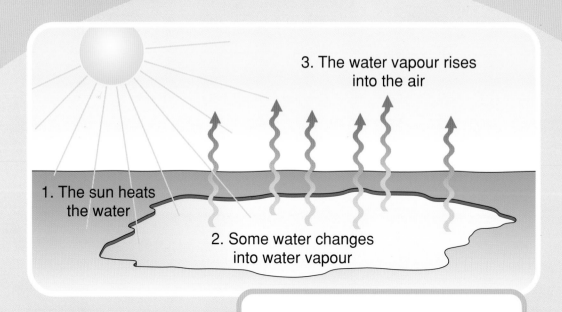

3. The water vapour rises into the air

1. The sun heats the water

2. Some water changes into water vapour

The way in which liquid water changes into a gas when heated is called **evaporation**.

When water vapour rises high in the air, it cools down. It becomes tiny **droplets** of water again. The droplets form clouds in the sky.

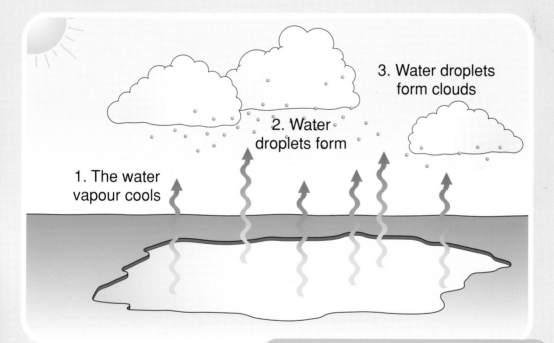

3. Water droplets form clouds

2. Water droplets form

1. The water vapour cools

The way in which water vapour changes into water droplets is called **condensation**.

The water cycle

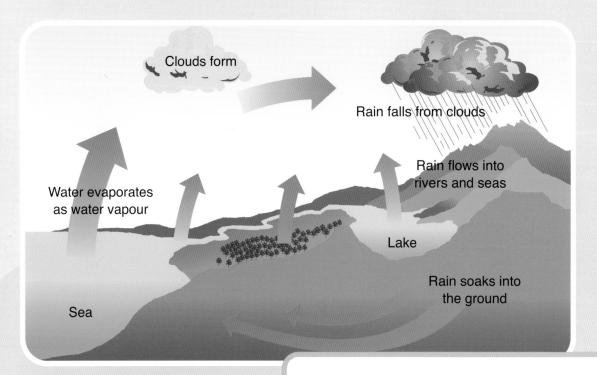

Clouds form

Rain falls from clouds

Rain flows into rivers and seas

Water evaporates as water vapour

Lake

Rain soaks into the ground

Sea

Water is moving around the water cycle all the time.

Rain is part of the water cycle. The water cycle is the way water keeps rising into the air as **water vapour** and falling again as rain.

In the water cycle, rain falls onto the land and into the sea. It fills rivers and lakes. Some rain soaks into the ground. It joins all the other water around us.

Rain runs into rivers. Rivers take rainwater to lakes and the sea. All this is part of the water cycle too.

Different kinds of rain

Raindrops can be small or large. Small raindrops make drizzle or light rain. The raindrops in drizzle can be as tiny as bits of dust.

Even the small raindrops in drizzle can make us wet.

When raindrops fall on water they make round patterns.

Sometimes lots of large raindrops fall.
This is called a downpour or heavy rain.
Raindrops in a downpour can be bigger
than garden peas.

Rainfall around the world

This map shows how much rain falls over a year, in different parts of the world.

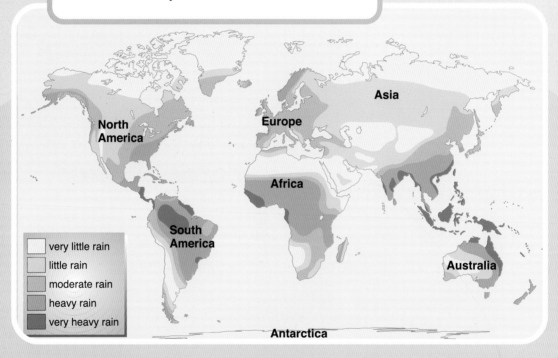

- very little rain
- little rain
- moderate rain
- heavy rain
- very heavy rain

North America

Europe

Asia

Africa

South America

Australia

Antarctica

The amount of rain that falls in a year is called the annual rainfall. In some parts of the world there is lots of rain. In other parts, there is hardly any rain.

Rain can fall in a special way near mountains. When air blows up a mountain it cools down. **Water vapour** in the air turns to rain. By the time the air blows down the other side of the mountain, it is dry.

The dry side of a mountain is called the **rain shadow**. Little or no rain falls here.

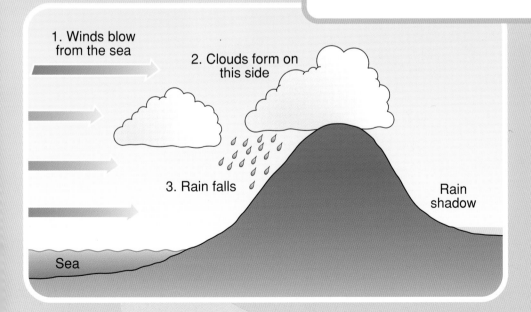

1. Winds blow from the sea

2. Clouds form on this side

3. Rain falls

Rain shadow

Sea

Rain and the seasons

Many places have two seasons: a dry season and a rainy season. In the dry season there is little or no rain. The rainy season brings plenty of rain.

People are often happy when the rainy season starts because it means the end of a long, hot summer.

In winter, sometimes the air is so cold that **snow** falls instead of rain.

Some parts of the world have four seasons: winter, spring, summer and autumn. It can rain in any season.

Who needs rain?

Everyone needs rain to stay alive. Rain brings the water that people drink. People also need rain to grow **crops**.

Many people around the world eat rice every day. Rice needs lots of water to grow.

Water in reservoirs is cleaned before it is pumped through pipes to your home.

When rain falls to the ground, some of it washes into drains. These carry the water to **reservoirs** and lakes. The water in your taps probably comes from a reservoir.

Plants in the rain

Plants need water to live. Lots of plants grow in places where there is plenty of rain. Thousands of plants grow in the **rainforests** of South America.

Lots of rain falls in rainforests like this. Trees here can grow higher than a 10-storey building!

When a place does not get enough rain for a long time it is called a drought. Many plants can die in droughts. If **crops** die, people may have nothing to eat.

A farmer has nothing to sell when his crops die in a drought.

Animals in the rain

Just like people, animals need rain to live. Many animals leave their homes when there is no rain. They travel a long way to places where they can find water.

Many animals gather to drink at pools of water like this one in Africa.

Slugs come out to feed on plant leaves after it has rained.

Some animals need the damp weather that rain brings. Slugs need to keep their bodies wet. In dry weather, they hide away under the ground.

Floods

Rain can cause floods. When lots of rain falls in a short time, rivers can fill up. The rainwater then spills out over the land.

People trapped by a flood may have to climb on to the roofs of cars or houses to escape.

These houses are high off the ground to protect them from floods.

In parts of Asia, heavy rain often causes floods. Some houses are built on wooden legs called stilts. This means that they are safer when the floods come.

Acid rain

Rain that carries **pollution** is called acid rain. Most of the pollution comes from factories and power stations. It mixes with **water vapour**, and makes acid rain in the air.

Pollution from chimneys mixes with the air.

Over several years, this stone wall has been worn away by acid rain.

Over time, acid rain can damage stone buildings and statues. Acid rain can also fall in lakes. This can spoil the water for the fish so that they become ill or die.

Project: rain diary

Find out how much rain falls where you live. To measure rainfall you need a rain gauge (you say, 'gage'). This is how you make one.

1. Ask an adult to help you cut the top off the drinks bottle.
2. Take the bottom part of the bottle and use a ruler to draw a line up the outside.
3. Add small marks and the numbers 0 to 5, at centimetre gaps along the line. This is your rain gauge.

4. Dig a small hole in the ground outside. Stand the rain gauge in it.
5. Put the top part of the bottle, upside down, in the gauge. This will help collect the rain.
6. Check the bottle each day. Write down how much rain is in it. Then empty out the water.
7. Look at your rain diary after a week. Which day had the most rain?

There is 5 cm of rain in this rain gauge.

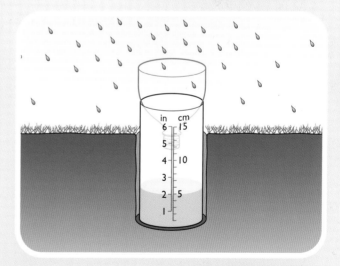

Find out more about rain at
www.heinemannexplore.co.uk

Glossary

condensation when water changes from a gas (water vapour) to a liquid

crops plants that farmers grow for food, such as vegetables or rice

droplets very small drops of a liquid such as water

evaporation how water changes from a liquid to a gas (water vapour)

gas does not have a solid shape and cannot be poured like water. The air is a gas.

pollution smoke or dirt that can damage the water, land and air around us

rainforest thick forest that grows in hot rainy places

rain shadow dry side of the mountain that does not get much rain

reservoirs lakes where water is kept for people to use

snow in very cold air, water droplets in clouds turn from liquid to solid and fall as snow

water vapour water that is part of the air. Water vapour is a gas that we cannot see.

Find out more

More books to read

Nature's Patterns: The Water Cycle, Monica Hughes (Heinemann Library, 2004)

My World of Science: Water, Angela Royston (Heinemann Library, 2001)

Geography Starts Here! Weather Around You, Angela Royston (Hodder Wayland, 2001)

What is Weather? Rain, Miranda Ashwell and Andy Owen (Heinemann Library, 1999)

Websites to visit

http://www.weatherwizkids.com
A website packed with information about weather features, satellite images from space, games and fun activities to do with the weather.

http://www.planetpals.com/weather.html
Learn more about different sorts of weather and interesting weather facts to share with friends.

Index

acid rain 26–7
animals 22–3
annual rainfall 14

clouds 6, 9, 10, 15
condensation 9, 30
crops 18, 21, 30

downpour 13
drizzle 12
drought 21

evaporation 8, 30

floods 24–5

mountains 15

rain gauge 28–9
rainforests 20, 30
rain shadow 15, 30
rivers 10, 11, 24

seasons 16–17

water cycle 10–11
water vapour 8–9, 15, 26, 30

Titles in the *Watching the Weather* series include:

Hardback   0 431 19022 4

Hardback   0 431 19023 2

Hardback   0 431 19024 0

Hardback   0 431 19025 9

Hardback   0 431 19026 7

Find out about the other titles in this series on our website www.heinemann.co.uk/library